T0209847

Twenty-One
Writings from the Heart to Motivate, Encourage, and Inspire

Delores P. Chavis

WESTBOW
PRESS®
A DIVISION OF THOMAS NELSON
& ZONDERVAN

WestBow Press books may be ordered through booksellers or by contacting:

WestBow Press
A Division of Thomas Nelson & Zondervan
1663 Liberty Drive
Bloomington, IN 47403
www.westbowpress.com
1 (866) 928-1240

ISBN: 978-1-9736-5046-1 (sc)
ISBN: 978-1-9736-5048-5 (hc)
ISBN: 978-1-9736-5047-8 (e)

Library of Congress Control Number: 2019900291

Print information available on the last page.

WestBow Press rev. date: 01/11/2019

Twenty-One Writings from the Heart speaks to whatever you're going through no matter where you are in the journey of life. Dee shares inspiring stories from her heart in a clear and easy way to understand. This book helps you understand God's love and plan for your life in a deeper way. *Twenty-One Writings from the Heart* challenges us to experience God's presence in everyday life where we work, live, or play.

—Chandra Moyer, coach, author, speaker

Twenty-One Writings from the Heart is easy reading. As I read, I felt a sense of calm, comfort, and inner peace. I kept seeing myself in each writing. It was as if God had me on His mind when He spoke to Delores. Truly a God-inspired book!

—Rev. Joyce L. Carcana

In an age and time when many are searching for a greater understanding of God and His Word, *Twenty-One Writings from the Heart* provides a compilation of writings that encourage us to see and seek God in all areas of our lives. The writings are clear and thoughtful, written with a simplicity that allows each reader to relate to the author's message.

—Rev. Warren E. Amlet, pastor

To my son, Stephen, who God gave to me just at the right time to keep me from self-destructing.

To my granddaughter, Zoe, who helped me experience all the wonderful things about child growth that I missed when raising my son.

To those seeking to know Father God in more practical ways.

Contents

Acknowledgments

I am very grateful and appreciative to those God put in my life to encourage me, pray for me, and keep me grounded in His care and purpose. To the women of SEE Ministries who are still standing by and with me, to the new friends I have been given since moving to North Carolina, and to my son, Stephen, who has been a steady source of encouragement, thank you! I want to also acknowledge the help and support of Phoenicia Warner of Wordd Enterprises, who helped with the first round of editing and kept down the level of frustration in this endeavor. To my brothers William and Henry for giving me the starting gift and confidence to move forward with this project. To those whose names I don't mention but who know me well enough to know my heart and sincerity, you are not forgotten but appreciated in very special ways. Bless you!

Introduction

To what extent do you want to experience an awesome walk with Father God? Not one orchestrated by the guidelines of others but one led by the Holy Spirit. The writings in this book and the scriptures given with them can help start you in that direction, or in some cases, refresh and pick up again. What you get from these writings and where the Holy Spirit will take you depends on you and your hunger for Him.

First John, chapter 2, verse 20 speaks of an anointing inside of us that allows us to know all things. That anointing is the Holy Spirit. He will teach us. He will also guide us. I can attest to that from personal experience. My spiritual training for the first twenty to twenty-five years excluded the knowledge of Jesus and the Holy Spirit. When I began to question that and seek more about them, I had no one to help or guide me in that quest. My total dependence was on God. I actively looked for someone to mentor me but to no avail. When I read the Bible, my understanding came from questioning God and rereading until He gave me understanding to go further. I would tell Him audibly when I didn't understand. Once I realized that I was being heard and listened to, a relationship of trust began. The books I read were books purchased by the leading of the Holy Spirit. Music I purchased was prompted by the Holy Spirit. I didn't know what to read or listen to, so I depended on Him to show me. Even though later in my life I attended seminary classes, what I received there in no way measured up to what I have learned from my relationship and dependence on the guidance and direction of the Holy Spirit.

I remember one situation where I needed a raincoat. I had a limited amount of money to use for it, and I knew exactly what I wanted, even the color. So, I enlisted the help of the Holy Spirit and asked Him to lead me to the coat. Down to the mall I went. The first store I entered, I found the coat. The price was within my budget, and it was the color I desired. But what did I do? I wanted to see if there was something else in another store. I went to every clothing store in that mall before I ended up back at the first one. That experience sealed the trust question for me. I heard in my spirit the Holy Spirit say, "Didn't you believe I was going to show you what you asked for?" There were other times it was evident that my relationship was being molded by God Himself. I was growing by His design, learning things He knew I needed to know. I think Father God recognized my sincere desire to know Him and my need for Him in my life.

Our dependence must be on God. There is no other way. He will send the people, open the doors, provide the resources, and map the way for us to proceed along the path He has for us. What you will read in this book are a few things Father taught me. My belief is that God gives us good things to share with one another, things to encourage one another in our growth as His representatives here on earth. We all have a part to do, something to share. Nothing is too small or unimportant in Father God's eyes if it is to glorify Him. I pray that as you read, study the scriptures, and record your thoughts and growth in your relationship with God, you will see the daily and practical ways He is moving and revealing Himself to you. See God in everything. Every place and activity is a classroom for learning, but you must be open and sensitive to receive it.

One of the most awesome things I learned as my relationship with Father God grew was that He communicates with each of us in a way He knows we will understand. We each respond to different ways of learning. God knows how to get our attention, and He knows our level of understanding. That is simply because He made us. There is something in each of us that is unique to our personal relationship with Father God. I call it PCS, personalized communication style. It was not long after taking time to reflect on how I usually heard Him that I recognized the PCS God uses with me. Doing that made me more sensitive and tuned in to hearing His voice and realizing just how often He speaks and is involved with my daily activities. I would encourage you to investigate that unique style God uses to communicate with you. What is it that He uses to get your attention? What makes your relationship with Him different from anyone else's relationship?

The writings, scriptures, and recordings are designed to be used together to focus on specific areas. It is not a one-day process or just a twenty-one-day devotional model. Each writing is meant to be studied to exhaustion, studied until you have received all Father wants to give you pertaining to that area of focus before moving on to another writing. Include Father in your reading and studies, ask Him to show you any improvements needed in each area, and let Him work in you. Regardless of how long we have been walking with God, we sometimes need to take another look at ourselves and how we are doing in various areas. Don't allow yourself to get so deep spiritually that you stop seeing the practical workings of God in your life. Let your relationship grow by experiencing Father in the *everyday* classrooms of life.

What has been written here is what Father God inspired me to write, as a result of listening to Him and experiencing Him in ways I never expected. I pray that you will be blessed, motivated, and encouraged to experience God in practical ways that will exceed your expectations! Blessings!

I will lead blind Israel down a new path, guiding them along an unfamiliar way. I will brighten the darkness before them and smooth out the road ahead of them. Yes, I will indeed do these things; I will not forsake them. —Isaiah 42:16 (NLT)

Unfamiliar Ways

Have you ever panicked when things were changed from the way you *usually* do or see them? Maybe you had to take a detour from a regular route to an unfamiliar one, or maybe an expected outcome didn't materialize. In either situation, you could easily be caught off guard, which would create the need to regroup mentally and emotionally. In this situation, it would also be very important to get your head straight so that you could focus on the change without your emotions being in control and could keep the stress out. This happens even when God Himself is leading us into unfamiliar territory or situations. Let me share an experience I had.

I was traveling to Virginia from Champaign, Illinois, during a winter storm. It wasn't snowing hard enough to cancel the flight, but by the time we reached Detroit, the weather had gotten worse. Our flight was the last in line for takeoff, and the pilot informed us that we had to wait until the storm passed over us.

After a forty-five-minute wait on the tarmac, the pilot finally came on again to update us. The plan was to take us to Canada and then down to Norfolk, Virginia. To do that, we had to return to the terminal to get more fuel. By this time, I was beside myself.

I just knew that the plane was being hijacked and I was in deep trouble! (Don't laugh yet.) I texted my son to tell him what was happening, only to receive a "Wow!" response from him. I then texted my niece in Champaign, who I had been visiting. Her response was not encouraging either. The problem was that my geographical skills were not sharp enough for me to realize where we were in relation to Canada.

While taxiing back to the terminal, the pilot gave us the option of either staying on the plane or getting off and staying in Detroit to wait for the next flight to Norfolk. The catch was that the terminal was closing for the night; we were the last plane out of there! The other issue was I didn't know anyone in Detroit!

As I pondered getting off the plane, I realized that that option was no longer available because the plane had begun to taxi back onto the runway. I waited too long to decide. Can you imagine the turmoil, frustration, and agony of not knowing what I was in for? Well, the enemy was flooding my head with all kinds of thoughts. I asked the stewardess why we had to go all the way to Canada. The lady in front of me turned around and said in an annoyed tone, "We are right here at the border!" I had no idea, but I never even bothered to tell her that I wasn't speaking to her!

The next thing I did was what I should have done first. I quieted myself, bowed my head, and asked Father God to tell me what was going on.

His answer was one I was not expecting, but it was also one I will never forget. It gave me more than peace and comfort. It confirmed how He was teaching me in one of His various classrooms of life. Awesome!

He let me know that the main reason for my fear and concern was the *unfamiliar*. Father explained that there are times He will take us to a destination by a route that is different from the one we are familiar with. Our destination never changes. Only the way we get there changes. There are reasons we may not know, but we must trust Him in providing the best way for us to get there. He always has purpose in what He does.

I must tell you that after listening to Father, I could sit back and enjoy the trip home. It was the smoothest flight. The sky was beautifully lit with stars, and there was no turbulence or worry! (Nothing to do with my lack of knowledge in geography.) It is a lesson that I will always remember: *Don't stress out over the unfamiliar things that come into my life. Just ask Father to tell me what's going on.* It just might be another lesson that He wants to teach me, and I am now assured that His way is always the best way!

Father, thank You for taking care of Your children. Help us to always rest in the knowledge that You will never take us where we will be in danger, that You seek only the best for us, and that our job is to trust You. I pray that in all things I will seek Your understanding and guidance.

Study It

Scriptures for Study   Additional Scriptures Found

Psalm 32:8 (AMP)
Proverbs 3:5–6 (NKJV)
Psalm 16:11 (NKJV)
Proverbs 16:9 (NLT)

What I've learned about myself from this writing:

What things have changed:

How I see God in uncertain times:

Trust in the Lord with all your heart; do not depend on your own understanding, Seek His will in all you do, and He will show you which path to take. (Proverbs 3:5–6 NLT)

Storm Sense

When my son, Stephen, first moved to North Carolina, I made sure to visit him wherever he lived. As young people often do, he moved from apartment to apartment, with different people, until he was able to get his own place. My purpose for visiting Stephen was not only to see him but also to see what environment he was in and by whom he was surrounded.

Just before making one of my planned visits, I heard the forecast of an approaching storm. Because the storm was coming my way from the south, I decided to wait until it passed before venturing out, even if it meant waiting until the next day. I can't exactly say that I was comfortable with that decision, and I couldn't figure out why. As I settled in, I decided to hold off on packing my bags and just relax. Soon, the Lord began to speak to me about my decision to wait. The first question He asked me was if I trusted Him. "Of course, I trust You, Father," I said. He replied, "Then what are you afraid of?" I didn't look at it as being afraid, but maybe I was. So I decided to prove that I trusted Father God and left for Durham, North Carolina. After all, it was only a three-hour drive.

The drive was going well, but soon I could see in the distance the storm that had been forecast. It was quickly approaching. I tried not to panic or get nervous and managed to hear the Lord speak to me. There was something He wanted to share with me. That was not the first time He used the practical everyday things to teach me something I needed to know. He often used the most unexpected places as classrooms! The first thing He wanted me to do was to accept and acknowledge the oncoming storm. There was no doubt that I was headed right for it. Then He said He wanted me to look around and observe who and what was around me as I approached the storm. *Why? What difference could it possibly make?* I thought.

As Father explained, it makes a big difference *who* is around you when you are going through a storm. As for *what* was around me, that made a difference too. Was there a place of safety? Somewhere to pull over if needed?

When I finally took notice of the vehicles around me, I saw a motorcyclist, a couple in a car driving seemingly at a safe, steady speed, and one more car that kept moving in and out of traffic. I was told to position myself, based on who was on the road with me, so I would feel and be safe as I went through the storm. I usually don't like to drive behind motorcycles, even in good weather, so I passed the motorcycle and got in front of it. I was okay with the couple, but the driver moving in and out of traffic was a distraction to me. If visibility got bad, I didn't want to be guessing where and when he would be moving. I decided to drive slower so that he could pass me and create a safe distance between us. I then felt in a good position to safely drive through the storm.

What did I learn from that experience? I learned that as I go through life, I will experience many storms—not just storms caused by nature but also the storms of life. Knowing who is with us in a storm is important. Are they there to help or hinder? Will they be liabilities or assets? Can I trust them to be steady and dependable in the storm? Is there a place of safety to weather the storm, if needed? All these are things to watch for and consider, especially when you see the storm approaching and have time to prepare.

God places people in our lives during certain seasons. We must learn to be sensitive to whether they are there to help us weather the storms that we encounter from time to time. He wants us to be prepared, but most of all, He wants us to know we can trust Him to get us through the storm.

Father, I praise Your holy name! I thank You for Your continued guidance as I walk this walk of faith in You. Continue to keep me close and to teach me in ways I understand. I am Yours, and I trust Your divine guidance.

Study It

Scriptures for Study   ·   Additional Scriptures Found

Psalms 56:10–11 (NLT)
Isaiah 26:3–4 (AMP)
Habakkuk 3:17–19 (NKJV)

What I've learned from this reading:

What things have changed:

Thoughts on Father God's concern for me:

This is the Lord's doing, and it is wonderful to see.
This is the day the Lord has made. We will rejoice
and be glad in it. (Psalms 118:23–24 NLT)

When Things Come to a Stop

✤

This morning was a particularly pleasing and peaceful morning. I awoke to the beauty of a snow-covered environment. The trees were coated, my car was covered, and the rooftops and streets were blanketed. It was everywhere. The snow was basically undisturbed, with exception of a few light footprints that had been made on the sidewalk before it stopped falling.

I went to my back window, opened the blinds, and let out a childish scream. It was a beautiful sight. My heart was light, and I began to sing and exclaim the goodness of the Lord. As I went to the front of the house, the scene was even more exciting. By that time, I imagined that others might have been viewing the snow as a problem. No one could safely move about in their cars, it was cold, and everything was shut down. But what a perfect opportunity to be still and reflect on the good and peaceful things for a while! Every day, we are bombarded by bad news, crazy politics, worries about things that we can't change, and all kinds of injustices and hurtful acts that people do to one another.

Sometimes, it even feels like there is more bad news than good. As I took in the beautiful sight of the snow that day, I decided to take the time to be still and enjoy the peace offered by Father God, even if it was just for one day.

Every now and then, there is a need to let everything come to a complete stop—a time to be still and acknowledge the work and power of our holy Father. During those times, we can release all our worries and concerns, relax in His presence, sing a song of joy, and get back to a place of peace and contentment. If we begin to look at the times when everything comes to a stop differently, changing our perspective, we will appreciate these days more. Living in these times of immediate access, we need more downtime. We could use more time to regroup, reflect, and remember the goodness of the Lord. After all, He is the one who controls our universe and our lives.

While writing this, I have noticed the brightness of the sun slowly melting the snow. He even knows how long of a rest we need. The next time everything comes to a stop, see it as Father God providing you with a time to be refreshed in His presence.

Father, teach us to recognize the times to get refreshed and rested. Help us to acknowledge and appreciate moments and days prepared just for us to enjoy Your presence.

Study It

Scriptures for Study   Additional Scriptures Found

Psalms 24:1–2 (NKJV)
Psalms 66:4–5 (NLT)
Mark 6:31 (NLT)
Psalms 23:1–3 (NKJV)

What I've learned about myself from this writing:

What things have changed:

How I recognize God's times for me to get refreshed and rested:

Delores P. Chavis

Let us hold fast the confession of our hope without wavering, for He who promised is faithful. (Hebrews 10:23 NKJV)

No Doubt

There are things we already know, but every now and again, we need to be reminded of them. In 1982, I was in the process of buying my first home in Virginia. While out one Friday night with my son for pizza, I discovered that my checkbook was missing. My need to find it resulted in us taking the pizza home to eat, which upset my son greatly. Once I got home, I found the checkbook on the kitchen counter and proceeded to share the good news with my son. Stephen was ten years old at the time and had recently given his life to the Lord. His response to all that had taken place was a *reminder* from Father to me! He calmly said, with a hint of accusation, "God's been good to you so far. What makes you think He's going to stop now?" While I stood there with my mouth open, wondering if I should pop him in the mouth, he added, "Instead of worrying, you should have had a little faith."

Well, what could I have said to that, other than, "You know, baby, you are right." Stephen is now in his forties, but I have never forgotten that reminder. Every time I even begin to doubt that Father God will come through in a situation, I am reminded of His words through my son that day.

We should never doubt the things we already know or the things that God has already proven about His character. He does not change. Be mindful of His sovereignty. We often find ourselves in situations that cause us to doubt whether God is aware of our need. When that happens, we must go to the Word of God and be reminded of His promises to those who love and obey Him. Be encouraged to know that the Almighty God is still concerned about you. Therefore, there is no need to doubt, because His hand is continually moving on your behalf.

Precious Father, I thank You for Your faithfulness to me. I acknowledge that I forget sometimes that You never change. Keep me close and always in remembrance of how much You love me.

Study It

Scriptures for Study   Additional Scriptures Found

Hebrews 10:23 (AMP)
Malachi 3:6 (NLT)
Psalm 89:34 (AMP)
1 Corinthians 1:9 (NLT)
Philippians 1:6 (NKJV)

What I've learned from this writing:

What things have changed:

Some things I need to be reminded of:

When he arrived and saw the grace of God [that was bestowed on them], he rejoiced and began to encourage them all with an unwavering heart to stay true and devoted to the Lord. For Barnabas was a good man (privately and publicly—his godly character benefitted both himself and others) and he was full of the Holy Spirit and full of faith (in Jesus the Messiah, through whom believers have everlasting life). And a great number of people were brought to the Lord. (Acts 11:23–24 AMP)

Encouragers Needed

While listening to one of my favorite speakers, I heard something I had not thought about before. As he delivered his sermon one Sunday morning, he explained that we all needed a Barnabas in our lives. With much explanation, he went on to say, that we needed a Paul and a Timothy too. As he described the characters of these biblical men and their impact on others, I realized that of the three, the one I needed the most during that season of my life was a Barnabas. The name Barnabas means *son of encouragement*. In a time when most people focus on themselves, having someone who encourages is much needed: a person who will be honest; who will tell us the good, the bad, and the ugly, in love; who looks out for our best interests and will always be there for us.

For most of my life, I had been seeking a mentor, someone to guide me along this spiritual walk and speak into my life. One day, as I shared this desire and my dismay over not having had any success in my search, my friend's husband offered a solution. It was simple. "Be a mentor to others." I cannot truly say I received that solution with joy when he first said it, but over time, I realized that others were probably feeling the way I did and having the same desire I had. At that point, I decided that I could be of help to others. That conversation took place more than fifteen years ago, and even though I never had a mentor, I was blessed to be used to encourage others in various ways over the years.

We should never underestimate the full impact we can have on others by simply giving them a smile or an encouraging word. Sometimes it might be that we need to take the time to listen to them, ask how they are, or show genuine interest in what they are doing. The same feelings we have, others have too. I have found that there is much satisfaction in giving what we need to someone else. When we do, our needs seem so much smaller and often disappear.

Having more encouragers would make our world a better place. With the growing use of social media, genuine relationships are not easily maintained. Today's conversations are usually conducted through text messages, emails, or some other type of social media. As a result, there is little eye contact made when communicating. To have a Barnabas relationship with someone, we must really get to know them, person to person. It might require more effort on our part, but it is worth the extra time and energy. This is a great way to *invest in people,* and when we make an investment in someone or something, we expect to receive a return. Just as Father God has invested the gift of love in us, I believe that a part of His return is seeing us use that love toward our brothers and sisters, through encouragement.

I encourage you to pray for God to send a Barnabas into your life, if you do not already have one—someone who will be an encourager to you. But even more, pray that He will show *you* how to be a Barnabas in someone's life.

Father, I thank You for Your Son, Jesus, who is the greatest encourager to us all. I pray that we will continually look up to Him as our example. As we learn to love and support one another, help us remember that we are our brothers' and sisters' keepers. Keep us humble as we go through each day and make us a blessing to those You put in our path daily.

Study It

Scriptures for Study   Additional Scriptures Found

Acts 9:26–28; 11:21–26 (NKJV)
Romans 1:11, 12 (NKJV)
Hebrews 13:1–3 (NLT)
1 Corinthians 13:4–7 (NLT)

What I learned from this writing:

What things have changed:

My Barnabas is:

I am a Barnabas to:

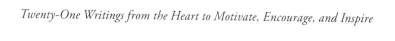

Once more Jesus addressed the crowd, He said, "I am the light of the world. He who follows Me will not walk in the darkness but will have the Light of life." (John 8:12 AMP)

Staying in Alignment

Have you ever been driving or riding in a car and noticed that the vehicle in front of you looked crooked? The first time I experienced that, I was amazed that such a crooked vehicle could go forward. When I inquired, I was told that the car needed an alignment. I could understand that, because I have had to get a physical alignment by a chiropractor. As I pondered the thought of being out of alignment physically, I wondered what being out of line spiritually was like. What does it look like to be out of alignment spiritually?

An interesting thought came to mind, and I was motivated to look at the phenomenon of an eclipse. An eclipse is when either the earth or the moon comes between the sun and the other planet, obscuring light from the sun and casting a shadow, causing complete or partial darkness. Both the earth and the moon depend on the sun for light and life. It's good to know that these eclipses do not last very long or occur too often. When objects or things come between us and the Son (Jesus), there is an eclipse—a spiritual eclipse. When we are not being guided by or walking by the biblical standards of Christ, we are out of alignment, and we

Delores P. Chavis

are walking in darkness (John 8:12). Remember, Jesus is the light. We have no light of our own.

Light is defined as illumination, daytime brightness, exposure to truth. *Nelson's New Illustrated Bible Dictionary* defines it as the opposite of darkness. The Bible speaks of light as the symbol of God's presence and righteous activity. Light also symbolizes the redemptive activity of God—goodness, holiness, salvation, and purity, to name a few. We need to be aligned properly with the Son. We cannot allow anything or anyone to come between us and the Son, blocking His light from shining through us.

What are some things that can get us out of alignment? Here are a few things to consider: unforgiveness, adultery, disobedience, pride, idolatry, greed, anger, and other people. Just as a natural eclipse can be predicted by astronomers, a spiritual eclipse can be predicted. When we begin to distance ourselves from the body of Christ, when we stop praying as often and procrastinate instead of studying God's Word, when we start listening to and associating with the wrong people, and when we stop loving others as we have been commanded to do (1 John 2:11), these are only a few signs that we are getting out of alignment and not in position to receive the life-giving light of Christ. Unlike the natural eclipse, a spiritual eclipse can be controlled to some extent. It will last for as long as we let it last. When we are aware that we are out of line with the Son, it is up to us to correct the situation (Ephesians 5:1–20). Let's not walk in darkness or out of alignment with the Son. Let the light of Christ be reflected to others through you (Matthew 5:14–16).

Father God, keep me alert and aware of my alignment with You, Your Word, and Your purpose for my life always. If, at any time I move either to the right or to the left, allowing something between me and Your light, give me the wisdom to realign myself quickly. And as Your light shines on me, embolden me to be a light for others that they may glorify You.

Study It

Scriptures for Study   Additional Scriptures Found

John 1:1–5 (NKJV)
Romans 13:12 (NLT)
1 John 1:5–7 (NKJV)
Psalms 27:1 (NKJV)
Psalms 1:1–2 (NKJV)

What I've learned from this writing:

What things have changed;

What it feels like and means to practice staying in alignment with God's will for me:

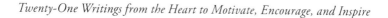

Don't copy the behavior and customs of this world, but let God transform you into a new person by changing the way you think. Then you will learn to know God's will for you, which is good and pleasing and perfect. (Romans 12:2 NLT)

A Sure Fit

I think we can all agree that a lot of the pain and frustration we experience in our lives is of our own doing and typically stems from a wrong fit. As a retired educator, I remember an activity I used in my first-grade class. It involved placing various shaped objects in slots that were identical in shape. Many of the children would try to put objects in the wrong slot, not knowing that only the same-shaped object would fit into the slot perfectly. So there were minutes of youthful force and frustration on their part as they tried to make the object fit into the wrong slot. Reactions varied from child to child. Some would move on to something else, some cried, and others continued to try to force a fit.

Likewise, as believers in Christ, we cause much pain and frustration for ourselves by trying to fit into places we don't belong, trying to be a part of things that are not fashioned for us. Pain and stress are caused by the friction of trying to make things fit in the wrong place. The more we wiggle and press, trying to fit in or be a part of something we shouldn't, the more pain and anxiety we experience. Like children struggling to force a fit where it doesn't belong, we often try hard to make things happen for ourselves. We want to maintain control and keep God from having total power and authority over our lives.

Why don't we fit into certain places and lifestyles? Consider the fact that we were not created for it. In other words, we were not shaped to be in that slot. As believers, we are to know that this world is not our home, as scripture reminds us that we are in the world but not of the world. If we keep this at the forefront of our hearts, we will not try to force ourselves into places, lifestyles, or habits that do not glorify God. Knowing and remembering what we were created for (Ephesians 2:10) and accepting God's purpose for our lives will help us to refrain from pushing, forcing, and wiggling ourselves into the wrong slots.

The ability to recognize our shape comes with Christian maturity. We don't have to force ourselves into shapes that aren't made for us. The Bible tells us exactly how we are to live and behave, but we must want that lifestyle. We will never experience a true fit until we accept and embrace the life that God has planned for us. How do we do that? We can start by seeking more of God, establishing a relationship with Him, and accepting His plans and purpose for us. We should read more of His Word, while striving to live the way He desires for us to live and being in fellowship with other believers. Doing these things will certainly be helpful. The ultimate misfit is a child of God trying to fit into the world when they have been shaped for His kingdom!

Father, show me Your way and reveal Your path and place for me, that I will walk in line with it. I pray that I will find peace in living for You and pursuing what will bring glory to You always.

Study It

Scriptures for Study   Additional Scriptures Found

John 15:19 (NLT)
Ephesians 1:5 (NLT)
2 Corinthians 6:14–18 (NLT)
Romans 12:2 (NKJV)
1 John 4:4 (NKJV)

What I've learned from his writing:

What things have changed:

How I feel about knowing where I fit:

Delores P. Chavis

For God speaks again and again, though people do not recognize it. (Job 33:14 NLT)

Seeing God's Messages

Over the weekend, I experienced a beautiful event that contained a message from Father God. I was not the only one experiencing this event, but I wonder how many others saw it as a message from Father God. We have been taught that we are to love—love God, love ourselves, and love our neighbors. We have heard that love conquers all, that love is kind, and that we are loved by God unconditionally. The event that I experienced was an event of love. The message I received from Father God was that He was showing us that love works, and we *can* live together in love and peace!

He used two people who fell in love. Two people from different countries, backgrounds, races, cultures, and childhood experiences. But they loved each other, and that love allowed them to overcome the differences in their lives. I believe they accepted the things they had in common and did not see the differences as things that would keep them apart. The focus was not on the negative but the positive. They loved each other.

As the world watched the wedding of Prince Harry of Britain's royal family and Meghan Markle of the United States, we saw history being made and changed. We saw two countries coming together to celebrate their love, and we saw races and social systems coming together sharing in it. We saw what the results of love could do, and I am sure that, like me, others were happy to witness such joy and happiness. To witness the acceptance of the things that two people, two countries, and two cultures had in common, forgetting the things that made them different, was nothing short of a miracle. They both chose to focus on their similarities, acknowledging that they could go forward, while accepting each other for who they were, and they did all of this in love.

Father God's message was that it can be done. We should continue to press forward in His love to make this world a better place, by accepting each other in love. When the news reports are full of chaos, killings, shootings, divisive reports, and so much negativity, remember we are all a part of making those things change. We must love this world into a better place, with His love as our example. For God so loved the world …

Lord, open ours eyes and our hearts to see and understand those things You show and reveal to us that help us know Your will and Your way for the earth. Let us learn the desires of Your heart and walk therein.

Study It

Scriptures for Study   Additional Scriptures Found

John 3:16, 17 (NKJV)
John 15:11–12 (NKJV)
1 Corinthians 13 (NKJV)
1 John 4:10–11 (NKJV)

What I've learned from this writing:

What things have changed:

Other ways I've noticed God communicating His desire for us:

Delores P. Chavis

So you, too, must keep watch! For you don't know what day your Lord is coming. Understand this: If a homeowner knew exactly when a burglar was coming, he would keep watch and not permit his house to be broken into. You also must be ready all the time, for the Son of Man will come when least expected. (Matthew 24:42–44 NLT)

Ready or Not, Here I Come!

⟨⟩⟨⟩⟨⟩

When I was a young child, I liked to play hide-and-seek. It is hard to tell if it is played much today, because of the amount of time children spend on their electronic devices. When I was growing up, many children frequently gathered in a big common area we called the yard and played outside for hours. Hide-and-seek was a favorite game. There was a person who was chosen as "it," and they had to stand facing the tree. As that person closed their eyes and counted to ten, everyone else scampered across the yard in search of a place to hide. Once they were done counting, the person who was chosen as it would yell loud enough for everyone to hear, "Ready or not, here I come!" The quest to find all the hiders would begin. If you were hiding and could get to the tree before the person who was it found and touched you, you were safe. The first one found and touched by "it" had to take their place. Finding a good hiding place was the key. It was always a good idea to make sure it was close by, because there was not much time to run to it. The only warning that was given was when the caller said, "Ready or not, here I come!" Not getting caught was a sign that you were good at finding places to hide.

There are times when Father God finds us in our hiding places as we try to run away from what He has told us to do, but as with so many in biblical times, we discover that there is no hiding from God. Remember Adam and Eve in the garden (Genesis 3:8)? They tried to hide from God, but they were found. Jonah was another one who tried to hide from God. He went through big efforts to run away from the assignment that God had given him (Jonah 1:1–3).

Sometimes we forget who God is when we try in our finite way to outsmart Him, but I imagine Him looking down on us, smiling and wondering when we are going to get it. He is omnipresent, which means He is everywhere (Psalms 139:7–10). He is omnipotent, which means He can do anything, because He has all power (Genesis 18:14). God is also omniscient, which means He knows all things (1 John 3:20). So, as the saying goes, you can run but you can't hide. Are you running? Trying to hide? I remember not wanting to be by myself, for fear of what I would hear Father God say to me. It might sound funny, but it is true. I didn't want to do or be what I knew He wanted me to do and be. I finally got the revelation and made the decision to govern myself accordingly, and I am so glad I did.

Father wants a relationship with us. He made us for His good pleasure (Philippians 2:13). He has plans for us (Jeremiah 29:11) that will allow us to live a fulfilled life. And most importantly, He wants us to be ready when His son Jesus returns. It is time to come out of hiding. You won't get the warning of "Ready or not, here I come!"

"So Always be ready, alert, and prepared, because at an hour when you're not expecting Him, the Son of Man will come" (Matthew 24:44 TPT).

Father, I want to be all You have called me to be. I want to fulfill the purpose You have for me in this world. Help me to boldly and humbly present myself to You. No hiding but willingly submitting myself to Your plans for me.

Study It

Scriptures for Study   Additional Scriptures Found

Jeremiah 23:23–24 (NKJV)
Acts 17:24–28 (NKJV)
John 14:3 (NKJV)
1 Thessalonians 4:16–17 (NKJV)
Hebrews 9:28 (NKJV)

What I learned from this writing:

What things have changed:

I think I'm ready because …

Have you never heard? Have you never understood? The Lord is the everlasting God, the Creator of all the earth. He never grows weak or weary. No one can measure the depths of His understanding. (Isaiah 40:28 NLT)

Been There...
Done That

❦

Recently, a close friend passed away—the second close friend I lost in a span of five months. They both were very close and dear to me, and the pain that I experienced, was unimaginable. The first was the result of a fatal car accident, and the other was a time-related situation, where doctors indicated that she had a longer time to live than what God decided. I was reflecting on the losses when Father God took the time to comfort me in a special way. As I was lying in bed, feeling sad and alone, Father reminded me of the story of Lazarus (John 11). It was then that I realized I was not the only one who had lost friends; Jesus lost a dear friend when Lazarus died. The thing that helped me was the way in which Father reminded me of a truth. I heard Jesus say, "Been there ... done that." In other words, He was saying to me, "Do not worry or be sad. I have your back, and I understand."

He helped me to remember that there is nothing we will ever go through that Jesus did not experience Himself. Greater yet, the Bible has recorded and helps us to see many examples of how

Jesus responded to similar experiences. Not only are we able to see how Jesus responded to various situations, but we can also take comfort in knowing that when we go to Him concerning anything, He truly understands. The Bible is a great gift, where God shows His undeniable love for us. In His Word, we can find everything we need to navigate through this life and many reminders that we are not alone.

You can probably remember times of distress, grief, or uncertainty in your life, when you just needed to know that someone understood what you were going through. Jesus experienced things here on this earth as a man, just as we are experiencing them. It is what makes Him our perfect high priest who intercedes on our behalf to the Father. He understands what it is like, living in this fallen world, and whenever we need to be understood and comforted, He is always there. Therefore, never feel that you are alone. There is someone who will always be there for you, if you go to Him. He cares, and He truly understands.

Father, I thank You for Your tender love, for knowing just what I need when I need it. Your understanding and comfort surpass all I've ever known.

Study It

Scriptures for Study | Additional Scriptures Found

Hebrews 4:14–15 (NLT)
John 16:33 (NLT)
Romans 15:4 (NKJV)
Deuteronomy 31:8 (NLT)

What I learned from this writing:

What things have changed:

Other things I have discovered about not being alone:

God decided in advance to adopt us into His own family by bringing us to Himself through Jesus Christ. This is what He wanted to do, and it gave Him great pleasure. So, we praise God for the glorious grace He has poured out on us who belong to His dear Son. He is so rich in kindness and grace that He purchased our freedom with the blood of His Son and forgave our sins. He has showered His kindness on us, along with all wisdom and understanding. God has now revealed to us His mysterious will regarding Christ- which is to fulfill His own good plan. And this is the plan: At the right time He will bring everything together under the authority of Christ—everything in heaven and on earth. (Ephesians 1:5–10 NLT)

Remembering Who God Is and What He Has Done

❧

Sometimes, we need to be reminded of the things we already know but have forgotten. Though our forgetfulness is not intentional, it sometimes takes a reminder to get us back to the things that are most important. For instance, we take friendships, relationships, and even family for granted. We fail to stop and be thankful for the little things that others do for us, and sometimes it takes a little reminder for us to remember the tremendous value of people in our lives.

Ephesians 1:5–10 reminds us of our Father God and how we sometimes forget who He is and all He has done and continues to do for us. As I stop and reflect on my life before I knew The Lord and His great love for me, I can't help but be thankful for the difference He has made in my life, and I never want to forget that. Ephesians 1:5–10 is such a beautiful part of scripture. In a simple but powerful way, this scripture gives us a look at the heart of Father God, who He is and what He desires for us. God first introduces Himself as *the* Creator. He isn't merely *a* creator; He is *the* Creator (Genesis 1:1–2). He wants you to remember that He made all things and that they were made for His glory and good pleasure—*even you.*

We get to see Him as a Father who adopts us into His own family, forgiving us for our sins. He did not spare the life of His only son Jesus to do so. He pours out grace and mercy freely upon us, showing kindness and daily providing His wisdom to us. Father God has also shared the mysteries of His plan regarding Christ fulfilling His purpose for all things in heaven and on earth. Think about it. It is all for His good pleasure, preplanned from the beginning of time. The king of glory wants us for Himself. He is a God who loves, a Father who embraces the welfare of His children, a God who provides and delights in those who are His. How often do you think about where you would be if His purpose did not include you? Or if His kindness and grace were suddenly withheld from you? Or if His wisdom was not available to you? Where would we be if He had been selfish and kept His *only* Son to Himself? Wow! Something to really think about, isn't it? I know that I would be in a most miserable state. However, when I stop and take time to remember, I remember how blessed I am and how much I am loved my Him.

I encourage you to take time daily to remember who our God is—*the* Creator of all things in heaven and on earth. Our Father and Creator. The One who loves us without conditions, who has plans for our success and shares those plans with us. We have been created for His good pleasure, so I think it is only fitting if we also make Him *our* good pleasure. May the richest blessings of our Father be upon you as you remember Him in all you do, allowing His presence to light up your day and bless you with His sustaining peace.

Father, I love You! I acknowledge Your awesome love for me. I am daily amazed and awed by Your continued care. I pray I will always remember and bless You with more of me in Your presence.

Delores P. Chavis

Study It

Scriptures for Study   Additional Scriptures Found

Genesis 1:26–31; 2:7, 18, 21–23 (NKJV)
Philippians 2:13 (NKJV)
Ephesians 1:5, 9 (NKJV)
Luke 12:32 (NKJV)
Jeremiah 1:5; 29:11 (NKJV)
Psalm 95:1–7 (NKJV)

What I learned from this writing:

What things have changed:

The things I try to remember daily about God are …

"As Jesus and the disciples continued on their way to Jerusalem, they came to a certain village where a woman named Martha welcomed Him into her home. Her sister, Mary, sat at the Lord's feet, listening to what He taught. But Martha was distracted by the big dinner she was preparing. She came to Jesus and said, "Lord, doesn't it seem unfair to You that my sister just sits here while I do all the work? Tell her to come and help me." But the Lord said to her, "My dear Martha, you are worried and upset over all these details! There is only one thing worth being concerned about. Mary has discovered it, and it will not be taken away from her." (Luke 10:38–42 NLT)

A Matter of Choice

Choices, choices, choices! Every day, we are required to make choices. Since the beginning of our existence, God has extended to us the *freedom of choice*. Whether or not we are aware, the choices we make are reflected in the lives we live. We choose where we will live, with whom we will associate, what type of books we will read, what kind of clothes we will wear, where we will worship, how much money we will spend, and for what we will spend it. We choose our mates, our friends, and a host of other things.

In the Bible, we read story after story about people who made choices. Some of them made were good choices, while others were not so good. For example, Adam and Eve each made a choice— first Eve, to take a bite of the forbidden fruit, and then Adam, to follow her lead (Genesis 3). Abram chose to obey God and left his country, family, and kinsmen (Genesis 12:1–5). Esau chose food over his birthright (Genesis 25:29–34). Jacob chose to work fourteen years for the wife he loved (Genesis 29:18–30). Esther chose to risk her life to save her people (Esther 3–8). David made a choice to wait for the promised kingship and not touch God's anointed (1 Samuel 26). Rahab chose to hide the spies (Joshua

2). Ruth chose to stay with Naomi (Ruth 1:3–22). Peter chose to deny Jesus three times (Mark 14:66–72). Paul chose to go through the trials, beatings, and stoning to know Christ (Acts 20:22–27). Judas made a choice to betray Christ (Luke 22:1–6; 47,48), and Jesus chose to die for us all (Matthew 26:36–44). Halleluiah!

Mary made a choice to take advantage of the precious time of learning from the Master, while Martha chose to focus on what needed to be done in the kitchen. Martha is often criticized for making that choice, but it is a good example of how we let circumstances cloud our ability to make the right choices sometimes. When making choices, we tend to overlook the spiritual benefits or consequences, only focusing on the natural outcome. This was the case with Martha, although, in her defense, two words can be interjected—responsibility and priority. It would be fair to Martha to recognize that she had some responsibilities to Jesus that she had prioritized above everything else. After all, it was her home that He was visiting that day. She took on the responsibilities of making sure His needs were met, that He was comfortable, and that he was properly fed.

Martha had a servant's heart and saw service to the Lord at that time as more important than receiving from Him. She chose to put serving first, while Mary chose to sit in His presence and receive. Like Martha, we often replace spending time with the Lord with the busyness of serving Him. We miss opportunities to be in His presence, to commune and develop our relationship with Him when we put less important things before Him. Jesus responded to Martha's complaint by explaining that Mary chose that good part! Webster defines the word *choose* this way: "To pick out by preference from what is available." In other words, she had a choice to either sit at His feet or go in the kitchen to help her sister. Likewise, we are constantly presented with choices, such as spending time in prayer, watching our favorite TV show, reading a few chapters in God's Word, or welcoming the invitation to run out to the mall with friends. No matter which way we go, it is a matter of choice.

You may ask, "Why was Mary's choice considered 'that good part'?" The first response that enters my mind is the scripture found in Matthew 4:4. When Satan was tempting Jesus to turn stones into bread, Jesus, also faced with a choice at that time, responded by saying, "Man does not live by bread alone, but on every word that comes from the mouth of God" (NKJV). In John 6:48, Jesus tells us that He is the bread of life. Mary chose to eat of the spiritual bread. She chose to feed her spirit self, which caused her to grow spiritually. She made a choice!

Think about the choices you make daily. Are they choices that will strengthen you spiritually and bring you into a more intimate relationship with Christ? Or are they choices that feed your natural or carnal self, ultimately satisfying the flesh? It is all a matter of choice, and by God's design, you get to choose!

> Two natures beat within my breast
> The one is foul, the one is blessed
> The one I love, the one I hate
> The one I feed will dominate
> —Tara Leigh Cobble

It is time to stop and reflect on the food you are eating and determine which of the two natures you are feeding the most. There is a saying: we are what we eat. It can also be applied to our spiritual lives. Is it time to change your diet? Only you can make that choice. Consider the life you are living. Are there choices you can make to better your life physically, spiritually, financially, emotionally, or relationally? Make a list of those choices and then prioritize them. Seek God's guidance and find a trusted friend to help you stay accountable in your efforts to make better choices.

Delores P. Chavis

Father, I thank You for the freedom of choice. Lead me now in making the choices that will bring me closer to You, knowing that it is in You that I will find peace, love, and joy to sustain me through each day.

Study It

Scriptures for Study   Additional Scriptures Found

Psalms 32:8 (AMP)
Colossians 1:9–11 (NLT)
Matthew 6:24, 33 (NKJV)
Psalms 119:102–103 (AMP)
Matthew 4:4 (NKJV)

What I learned from this writing:

What things have changed:

How I'm making better choices:

While a large crowd was gathering, and people were coming to Jesus from town after town, He told this parable: "A farmer went out to sow his seed. As he was scattering the seed, some fell along the path; it was trampled on, and the birds ate it up. Some fell on rocky ground, and when it came up, the plants withered because they had no moisture. Other seed fell among thorns, which grew up with it and choked the plants. Still other seed fell on good soil. It came up and yielded a crop, a hundred times more than was sown." When He said this, He called out, "Whoever has ears to hear, let them hear" … But the seed on good soil stands for those who with a noble and good heart, who hear the word, retain it, and by persevering produce a crop. (Luke 8:4–8, 15 NIV)

Fruit

When God created Adam and Eve, He gave them the command to be "fruitful and multiply" (Genesis 1:27–28). Jesus instructs us to make disciples in Matthew 28:19, which is a form of multiplying and producing fruit. The scripture used for this writing is relative to a popular parable that Jesus shared, referred to as the parable of the sower. In this parable, Jesus tells of a farmer sowing seeds and what happens when the seed falls on various kinds of soil. The soil determines if the seed will sprout, as well as the quantity and quality of fruit it will produce. As He often did, Jesus spoke this parable to His disciples and later explained what it meant. From His explanation, we understand the importance of both the soil and our perseverance. It is true that the soil is important, but we also must persevere in taking the necessary steps to prepare it, to receive the harvest that we desire to produce.

The first thing we need to consider is the soil. In this parable, the seed is the Word of God, and the soil is our heart. Our heart condition determines if the seed (Word of God) will take root and grow. Jesus described good soil as hearing and keeping the Word with a good and honest heart (Luke 8:15 ASV). As with our physical health, our heart plays an important part in being spiritually healthy. If we hear the Word of God with a good and honest heart, we will retain it better and eventually produce good fruit.

The second thing that affects our fruit is the effort we put into the growth process. The last phrase of verse 15 in the NIV translation says, "and by persevering produce a crop." Some translations use the word patience in place of the word persevering. However, I like the New International Version of that verse, because I am mostly challenged by the word *persevering*. Per *Webster's Dictionary*, to persevere means "to continue in some effort, course of action, despite difficulty or opposition etc.; to be steadfast in purpose; to persist." It is safe to say then that "maintaining" the good soil is where the perseverance comes in. Soil needs to be taken care of, watered and fertilized on a regular basis, or it will not be fit to produce a quality crop from the seed planted in it. How can I keep a noble and good heart? Am I reading, hearing, and retaining God's Word by putting it into practice daily? Am I still *good* soil? Am I persevering in the things that will help me keep an honest and good heart? These are questions I ask myself from time to time, and even though I cannot truly say that I always persevere as I should, I am certainly motivated to do better.

There are many distractions in our lives that compete for our attention daily. That is why our task is to keep our focus and maintain progress on those things that are most important and are in line with our purpose of being fruitful. Persevering is not always easy, but it is necessary to be successful in what we want to accomplish—a bountiful crop!

Have you tested the quality of your soil lately? If not, consider using these tips to help you to be and maintain good soil.

- Pray for focus.

- Make time for meeting with God daily.
- Read the Word daily.
- Get an accountability partner.
- Always pray for God's direction, grace, and wisdom for daily living.

Father, help me to stay focused on being productive in Your kingdom. Let my fruit be plentiful and lasting as I study Your Word, spend time with You, and keep a good and honest heart.

Delores P. Chavis

Study It

Scriptures for Study

Additional Scriptures Found

Psalms 1:1–3 (NLT)
Luke 8:11–15 (NKJV)
Ezekiel 36:26–27 (NLT)
Proverbs 4:23 (NKJV)
1 Chronicles 28:9 (NLT)
John 15:7–8 (NKJV)
John 15:17 (NKJV)

What I learned from this writing:

What things have changed:

My fruit before and after:

Can anything ever separate us from Christ's love? Does it mean He no longer loves us if we have trouble or calamity, or are persecuted, or hungry, or destitute, or in danger, or threatened with death? No, despite all these things, overwhelming victory is ours through Christ, who loved us. And I am convinced that nothing can ever separate us from God's love. Neither death nor life, neither angels nor demons, neither our fears for today nor our worries about tomorrow—not even the powers of hell can separate us from God's love. No power in the sky above or in the earth below—indeed, nothing in all creation will ever be able to separate us from the love of God that is revealed in Christ Jesus our Lord. (Romans 8:35, 37–39 NLT)

Handling the Adversities of Life

"If it's not one thing, it's another!" I know you have heard or made that statement before. Maybe you are even feeling that way right now. As I've gotten older, I've realized that life is made up of seasons and that each season has a shelf life. In other words, whatever season we find ourselves in will end at some point. For some of us, it might seem that we are *always* going through something, but as believers, we must be reminded that the Word of God tells us that in this world, we will have tribulation and trials (John 16:13). It also encourages us to not become frustrated, because Christ has overcome the world.

Having gone through many seasons of trials, I am now convinced that our perception of *who* we are, *why* we are, and *what* we are supposed to be doing plays a key role in how we view the adversities of this life. I believe that our perspective of what we go through is highly related to knowing our purpose. Consider *why* we were created (Philippians 2:13), *who* created us (Genesis 2:27), and *what* He has purposed for our lives (Jeremiah 29:11).

Everything we go through in this life, whether it feels good or bad, points to God our Father and His purpose for us (Romans 8:28).

Over the years, reading and studying God's Word, I have been blessed by the life of Paul and how he handled the many trials he faced. He showed a remarkable tolerance for enduring pain, hardship, trials, and tribulations. He continues to be an example and encouragement to me and many others. Paul understood his purpose. In Philippians 3:10, he shares that the understanding of his purpose was the thrust and motivating factor that allowed him to go through the many things he did. Paul's outlook on adversities and on life in general is quite interesting but can be challenging. He viewed circumstances in relation to eternity (2 Corinthians 4:17–18). That made a difference in his attitude toward the adversities he encountered. Paul knew the love of Christ and held fast to the promises of God.

Even though our problems are not necessarily the same as Paul's, because we are living in a different time, we should endeavor to see things in relation to both our purpose and eternity. We must remember that our adversary, the devil, is always looking to find ways to circumvent Father's purpose for us. We must also remember that God's Word reveals that through Christ, we already have the victory over our adversary and every adversity. It is also important to keep in mind how much we are loved and cared for, even in trials, lonely times, and hardships. There is never a moment when we are without Father's unconditional love. Therefore, when opposition arises and things get a little rough, continue to press forward, knowing that you are not alone. There is nothing that can separate us from His love. Be encouraged as you face the various hardships and adversities of this life, because they will never outweigh the love God has for you. Trust Him to bring you through. You can do all things through Christ Jesus, who strengthens you (Philippians 4:13).

Father God, I thank You this day that You are always with me. Your love never fails, and Your glory light ever shines, leading me to safety. Keep me close to You always! Let me be strong and steadfast to stay the course You have for me.

Study It

Scriptures for Study   Additional Scriptures Found

Romans 8:28 (NKJV)
Matthew 11:28–30 (NKJV)
2 Timothy 2:1–3 (NKJV)
Romans 8:18 (NKJV)
1 Peter 4:12–13 (NLT)
Isaiah 43:1–2 (NKJV)
1 Peter 5:8–9 (NLT)

What I've learned from this writing:

What things have changed:

Overcoming my latest obstacle:

Then he said to me, "Speak a prophetic message to the winds, son of man. Speak a prophetic message and say, "This is what the Sovereign LORD says: Come, O breath, from the four winds! Breathe into these dead bodies so they may live again."' So, I spoke the message as he commanded me, and breath came into their bodies. They all came to life and stood up on their feet—a great army. (Ezekiel 37:9–10 NLT)

Power to Change

❧

Change. Not many people receive change well (including myself) or are able to adjust to it quickly. And then there are those who simply roll with the punches or go with the flow quite easily. I used to think I needed to get ready for change—prepare myself, adjust my attitude, understand why the change was occurring, and know how it would better my situation. In other words, I wanted to be in control, even of the change. There is a change that can occur *in* us, and that change we have some say about. It is the transforming change that occurs when we allow Jesus into our lives. We have a choice in this matter; either we do or we don't accept Him. When we accept Jesus into our life, we become new creations (2 Corinthians 5:17–18). That is major change, and the benefits are awesome!

One Sunday morning as I sat in church listening to the sermon, I heard something that helped me understand feelings I was having about my spiritual condition. The pastor began to describe people he called "spiritual misfits." That was when I understood why I acted the way I did and that it was perfectly okay! As the pastor explained, misfits are those people who don't or can't settle for the status quo, and they are always seeking more.

They don't always fit in with the crowd and usually wonder why they feel like they are different. That was me! Now I understood why I always felt different and like an outsider. I was looking for change. I wanted to experience more spiritually. Father God had put a desire in me to not settle because He had so much more He wanted me to know and experience about Him. As I grew closer to God, I did experience and note the change in me, and the change continues. It's called being transformed (Romans 12:2 NLT).

I want to assure you that what God wants to do in your life by way of His Holy Spirit is well worth the change that will occur in your life. Do you want to change? Do you want to be transformed? Are you tired of the status quo and settling for what others think is enough? At what cost are you willing to allow change to take place? I suggest that we have good reason to embrace and desire this transformation, but it is our choice. If we want change and transformation, God will do it by His power through His precious Holy Spirit. The word "spirit" means *breath* or *wind*. Without going into a lengthy study of the Holy Spirit (which I strongly suggest you do), consider these scriptures for breath and wind as describing the Holy Spirit: John 20:22; John 3:6–8. In looking at the definition of the word "wind," I went to several sources. I found that the word wind refers to any natural movement of air, whether of high or low velocity or great or little force. There is a light wind we call a breeze; it's mild and fresh. There is a strong, somewhat violent wind we call a gale wind. Then there is that sudden, brief wind. It can come in a light puff we call a gust, or it may come in a driving rush that we call a blast—somewhat like the mighty rushing wind that came on the day of Pentecost (Acts 2:2). The wind has the power to change things. Strong winds can destroy and displace things; mild winds can refresh and revive. The Holy Spirit is strong enough to destroy those ungodly things and habits in your life yet mild and gentle enough to refresh, revive, and comfort you as you change. He dwells in us and was given by Father God as our helper. He is the best friend anyone could ask for.

Father, first I thank You for giving me the opportunity to change, to know that You alone will shower me with Your unconditional love and welcome me as I come to You. I thank You for Your precious Holy Spirit, who is here with me to help me on this journey of transformation into being more like Your Son, Jesus.

Study It

Scriptures for Study   Additional Scriptures Found

Jeremiah 18:1–6 (NLT)
Acts 2:1–4 (AMP)
John 20:22 (NKJV)
John 3:8 (NKJV)
Genesis 2:7 (NKJV)
2 Corinthians 3:18 (NLT)

What I've learned from this writing:

What things have changed:

How I feel about my change:

Blessed be the God and Father of our Lord Jesus Christ, who according to His abundant mercy has begotten us again to a living hope through the resurrection of Jesus Christ from the dead, to an inheritance incorruptible and undefiled and that does not fade away, reserved in heaven for you, ... Therefore gird up the loins of your mind, be sober, and rest your hope fully upon the grace that is to be brought to you at the revelation of Jesus Christ. (1 Peter 1:3—4, 13 NKJV)

Hope

King Solomon, who was the wisest man to live, wrote, "Hope deferred makes the heart sick, but when the desire is fulfilled, it is a tree of life" (Proverbs 13:12 AMP). What I concluded from that it hope is vital to life. Hope is defined as a feeling that what is wanted will happen; a desire accompanied by expectation. Hope can also be defined as a desire based on a promise of God, which communicates the certainty of God's blessings and encourages our souls. Simply put, hope is confident expectancy. There is a difference between natural hope and spiritual hope. The difference is the foundation on which one's hope is based. One songwriter wrote, "My hope is built on nothing less, than Jesus' blood and righteousness." There are many promises in the Bible that we as Christians base our hope on. Paul speaks of the hope of eternal life (Titus 1:2) and the hope we have in Christ Jesus (1 Timothy 1:1). A study of the Bible will reveal the many promises of God to His people and the hope that is there for believers. We believe that the promises of God are true. We believe that every promise will be fulfilled. We have hope in our future because we have hope in God.

Christian hope comes from God rather than from individual

desires or wishes. This distinguishes Christians from nonbelievers. Hope is from God and abides in each believer (1 John 3:3; 1 Peter 3:15).

As we look at hope and examine what it truly means, what does Father God want us to know? And what does He want us to do? God has made many promises to us, and according to Psalms 105:2, He is a promise keeper. There are times we forget that He has promised to always be with us, and we often think we are alone. We think that no one cares for us or about what we are going through. During those times, we have hope, because He promised that He will always be with us (Matthew 28:20). We should keep hope in that promise. God's desire is to give us hope and a future (Jeremiah 29:11). He has promised us peace that surpasses all understanding (Philippians 4:7), a peace that the world cannot take from us. God wants us to keep our hope in that peace (John 16:33). In Psalms 37:4, He promised that He would give us the desires of our hearts as we delight ourselves in Him. He wants us to keep our hope in that promise. Father wants us to keep our hope in the glorious reappearing of His Son, Jesus Christ. He wants us to keep our hope in His promise of eternal life.

One author wrote that hope is faith in seed form. As our hope is sustained and maintained, our faith grows stronger. When King David wanted relief from his adversaries, he wrote Psalms 71. In the fifth verse, he wrote this supplication to the Lord; "For You are my hope, O Lord God; You are my trust from my youth" (Psalms 71:5 NKJV). Although he was aging, his hope and trust was still in God. He puts it this way in verse 14: "But I will hope continually and will praise You yet more and more" (Psalms 71:14 NKJV).

God wants us to remember who He is and to have continued

hope in Him. Our attitudes should be like David, when he wrote Psalms 16:8–9.

"I have set the LORD always before me; because He is at my right hand, I shall not be moved. Therefore, my heart is glad, and my glory rejoices; my flesh also shall rest in hope" (Psalms 16:8–9 NKJV).

Father, I praise You for Your faithfulness to me. I thank You that Your promises are yes and amen!

Study It

Scriptures for Study   Additional Scriptures Found

Psalms 71 (NKJV)
Psalms 16:9–11 (NKJV)
Romans 8:23–26; 14:13 (NKJV)
Hebrews 6:19–20 (NKJV)
1 John 3:2–3 (NKJV)

What I've learned from this writing:

What things have changed:

My greatest hope:

Then I will pour water on you, and you will be clean; I will cleanse you from all your filthiness and from all your idols. Moreover I will give you a new heart and put a new spirit within you; and remove the heart of stone from your flesh and give you a heart of flesh. I will put My spirit within you and cause you to walk in My statues, and you will be careful to observe My ordinances. (Ezekiel 36:25–27 NASB)

New Life

It is always great when we can get a fresh new start. It gives us an opportunity to clean up our act and lead better lives. Things that didn't go so well before can be tossed out, giving us opportunities to make better decisions, based on what we have learned from our past experiences. Believe it or not, we are all given the opportunity to make a start each day and to walk in a newness of life. But what is life? In general terms, life can be described as that time between birth and death (*Nelson's New Illustrated Bible Dictionary*). But during that period, the word *life* can take on different meanings.

As a believer in the Bible, I accept the account in Genesis that explains that life comes from God (Genesis 2:7). Therefore, the newness of life refers to the new and eternal life we are offered through Christ Jesus (John 14:6). Although this new life is spiritual, it affects our physical and spiritual beings, and we decide whether we will have it or not. Because it is free, no one is ever forced to receive it. Isn't that something? We are given the opportunity to make a new start, and it doesn't cost us anything (2 Corinthians 5:17). We had no control over our physical birth, but we do have a say in our spiritual rebirth. If you think about it, it is not as difficult as it might seem. All it requires is a sincere decision that changes our lives for the better.

This new life is about relationship and the acceptance of the free offer of eternal life that we were given through Jesus Christ (John 3:16–17; 1:11–12; 1 John 5:11–12). When we accept the gift of new life in Jesus, our relationship begins with Him, Father God, and the Holy Spirit. Accepting the gift is a matter of belief. The New Living Translation puts it this way: "If you openly declare that Jesus is Lord and believe in your heart that God raised Him from the dead, you will be saved. For it is by believing in your heart that you are made right with God, and it is by openly declaring your faith that you are saved" (Romans 10:9–10 NLT).

God loves us so much that He provided a way for us to have new life, and with this new life comes a new nature and a new freedom. We can align ourselves with the will and ways of God by dying to the old nature and ways of the world (Romans 12:1–2 NLT). New life means accepting Jesus Christ, living for Him, and making Him first in our lives. It means dying to the concerns and standards of this world and looking to the eternal life we have in Christ Jesus. Life is beautiful! But life in Christ Jesus is awesome! It is where we find the abundance of life (John 10:10). You are never alone as you walk in the newness of life in Christ Jesus. Times are not always smooth and problem-free, but the promises found in God's Word (Bible) will sustain you on your journey (Hebrews 13:5–6).

Father God, because of Your love, we all have been given the opportunity to walk in the newness of life. I thank You for that and pray that my choice to do so will encourage others to seek You for themselves.

Study It

Scriptures for Study   Additional Scriptures Found

Isaiah 43:18–19 (NLT)
Colossians 2:20 (NKJV)
Psalms 32:8 (NKJV)
2 Corinthians 5:17–18 (NKJV)
John 3:5–8 (NKJV)

What I have learned from this writing:

What things have changed:

Benefits of a new life:

Delores P. Chavis

Mordecai sent this reply to Esther: "Don't think for a moment that because you're in the palace you will escape when all other Jews are killed. If you keep quiet at a time like this, deliverance and relief for the Jews will arise from some other place, but you and your relatives will die. Who knowns if perhaps you were made queen for such a time as this?" (Esther 4:13–14 NKJV)

Pushed to Action

I'm sure most people have heard the story of Queen Esther, how she became queen and the great courage she possessed to save her people. We can glean many lessons from the story if we explore the content from different perspectives. Take Mordecai's role, for example. If we look at his response to Esther, we see that it is worth paying attention to and remembering when it comes to our own lives. It would be a great idea to get acquainted with the entire book of Esther, but Mordecai's response to Esther in our scripture says a mouthful. It was a blunt and direct confrontation with Esther, which was quite different from their usual relationship. I'm sure it came as a surprise to Esther, but I'm also certain that it allowed her to realize the urgency of the matter at hand. Have you ever been confronted by a close friend? Like Esther, it may have come as a surprise, and perhaps it made you a bit uncomfortable. I'm sure it also made you stop and consider a lot of things about yourself and your actions. Do you remember what prompted that confrontation? Was it necessary? Did you feel that that friend was expecting too much of you? Did you see things the way your friend saw them in that situation?

No matter where we are in our lives or how we perceive

ourselves, we all have a God-given purpose. Sadly, we move forward on our path, focusing on ourselves, rather than remaining in tune with the perspectives of what Father God wants us to do. We must be diligent in remembering how important it is to keep in close relationship with Father God and the directions He constantly gives us. Rather than looking at the small picture, we need to see every assignment that He leads us into as our purpose, in relation to kingdom building. Can you see yourself as being used by God for major assignments? Whenever God gives us major assignments, we often think it is not something we are able to do. We usually doubt that we are gifted and anointed to do the task, because of certain limitations we put on ourselves. We convince ourselves we are not educated enough or that no one will listen to us, but let me stop and announce that those thoughts are ideas and suggestions the enemy has planted in our minds. The truth is we can do all things through Christ, who gives us the strength and ability to accomplish what we need to, according to Philippians 4:13. We must also remember that we are just the obedient earthen vessels that He uses and works through.

This is exactly what happened to Esther. With a strong reminder from Mordecai, she stepped up to the plate. As we meditate on Esther's actions, what can we learn from this? When we put limits on ourselves, we are limiting God and what He can do in our lives. We must always remember that there is nothing too hard for God (Luke 1:37) and that He is the one working His will through us.

Father, in all that I say or do, let me remember that it is You working through me. I will stay close to You and be ready for each assignment I am privileged to be given, to bring all glory to You. Thank You for using me!

Study It

Scriptures for Study   Additional Scriptures Found

Romans 8:28–29 (NKJV)
Philippians 3:12–14 (NKJV)
Philippians 4:13 (NKJV)
Jeremiah 29:11 (NKJV)
Proverbs 16:9 (NKJV)
Proverbs 3:5–6 (NKJV)

What I learned from this writing:

What things changed:

There is something I need to act on:

A certain woman of the wives of the sons of the prophets cried out to Elisha, saying, "Your servant my husband is dead, and you know that your servant feared the Lord. and the creditor is coming to take my two sons to be his slaves." So, Elisha said to her, "What shall I do for you? Tell me, what do you have in the house?" And she said, "Your maidservant has nothing in the house but a jar of oil." Then he said, "Go, borrow vessels from everywhere, from all your neighbors—empty vessels; do not gather just a few. And when you have come in, you shall shut the door behind you and your sons; then pour it into all those vessels and set aside the full ones." So, she went from him and shut the door behind her and her sons, who brought the vessels to her; and she poured it out. Now it came to pass, when the vessels were full, that she said to her son, "Bring me another vessel." And he said to her, "There is not another vessel." So, the oil ceased. Then she came and told the man of God. And he said, "Go pay your debt; and you and your sons live on the rest." (2 Kings 4:1–7 NKJV)

Positioned for a Miracle

Everyone stands in need of a miracle at one time or another. However, we can miss our miracles if we are not positioned to receive them. The Bible is filled with many accounts of miracles performed by God and some of His chosen servants. One that stands out to me is the miracle received by a widowed woman. We can learn from this story regarding being in position to receive. The story is found in 2 Kings 4:1–7. The woman wasn't given a name, but her story has great meaning for those looking for a miracle in their lives. Just as this widow in our story came to a place in her life where she needed a miracle, we too are finding that as things are so uncertain in this world, we need miracles. But are we positioned to receive our miracles? Just as this widow sought the man of God in her day, we have only one place to go for help, and that is to the one who holds all things in His hand—Christ alone.

Whenever we need help, we usually do one of two things. We try to work things out on our own, or we seek help from others. And in many cases, they are just as much in need as we are. We go to the wrong source for help. In this story, when the widow realized that she needed help, she immediately went to the one person she knew could help. We are admonished in Proverbs 3:5–7 that our trust should not be in our own ability but in God. Philippians 4:19 also reminds us that God will supply all our needs.

So just how do we position ourselves to receive from Father God? Let's look at what the widow did. The first thing she did was to acknowledge that she needed help. For some of us, that is a lot more difficult than it seems and is easier said than done. We don't want others to know that we are in need. We go around in denial, as if nothing is wrong, hoping and praying for God to intervene. However, like this widow, we need to humble ourselves and admit that we are in need. The second thing is that she didn't let pride get in the way of asking her neighbors for the jars, as the man of God directed her to do. Some of us have so much pride that we hesitate to give God the opportunity to send help through the people around us. And the last thing was that she was obedient to the instructions she received from the man of God. She didn't ask any questions or come up with any excuses; she willingly did as he told her to do.

There were two instructions given to the widow that I would like to expand on, because they are important to remember. In borrowing the jars, she was told, "do not gather just a few" (2 Kings 4:3 NKJV). The prophet was telling her that the more she anticipated and prepared for, the more she would receive. This indicates that the size of the miracle or blessing depended upon how big she believed. We sometimes want to put limits on what God can and wants to do. The oil only stopped flowing when there were no jars to contain it. Our miracle will only be as big as our faith. How big is your faith? Ephesians 3:20 tells us that God can accomplish infinitely more than we are able to ask or think. He is a God of more than enough.

The second thing she was told was also interesting. The

prophet of the Lord instructed her to "shut the door behind you and your sons" (2 Kings 4:4 NKJV). I wondered about this for a while, but soon the Holy Spirit helped me to understand. Sometimes we need to be separated from the outside world while Father God is working in and for us. He separates us so that we will not be distracted by the things going on around us. That is why we are instructed to close the door on those things that will hinder or delay our miracle. That is something to think about as you position yourself for your miracle. Acknowledge your need for a miracle, humble yourself and overcome any pride, be obedient to God, and then have big faith. Your miracle is on the way!

This story teaches us much more. I encourage you to dig deeper and take peace in knowing that God will supply your every need.

Father God, I thank You for being my bountiful source of all things. Help me to remember that You have plans for me to succeed and have a future. Let me always keep You as the center and focus of all I do.

Study It

Scriptures for Study   Additional Scriptures Found

Philippians 4:19 (NKJV)
Psalms 145:18–19 (NKJV)
Psalms 37:4–5 (NKJV)
Psalms 121:1–2 (NKJV)
Proverbs 3:5–7 (NKJV)

What I learned from this writing:

What things changed:

Getting ready for my miracles:

Oh, what joy for those whose disobedience is forgiven, whose sin is put out of sight! Yes, what joy for those whose record the Lord has cleared of guilt, whose lives are lived in complete honesty! When I refused to confess my sin, my body wasted away, and I groaned all day long. Day and night Your hand of discipline was heavy on me. My strength evaporated like water in the summer heat. Finally, I confessed all my sins to You and stopped trying to hide my guilt. I said to myself, "I will confess my rebellion to the Lord." And You forgave me! All my guilt is gone. (Psalms 32:1–2 NLT)

I am sure many of you have heard the acronym TGIF, especially if you are over the age of fifty. I am not sure what meaning is given to it now, but in my younger years, it meant *thank God it's Friday*! Friday. The end of the workweek, a time for relaxing and getting away. Usually, we would go out and party for a while before going home. Most of us enjoyed the liberty of doing something fun or different to let our hair down. Now that I have given my life to Jesus, I have changed the ways that I celebrate TGIF. In fact, I want to share a different meaning for that acronym, one that benefits all who believe in Jesus. To me, TGIF means *thank God I'm forgiven*!

In the thirty-second book of the Psalms, David does an excellent job describing what he felt like before and after being forgiven for his sins. Psalms 32 is called a reflective poem and is also what is called a *maskil*. Maskil is a psalm written to make a person wise or prudent or to increase a person's success or skill. The sin David was referring to is the one he committed against Bath-Sheba and her husband, Uriah (2 Samuel 11). David's experience with that sin and the gracious forgiveness he received from God prompted him to put those feelings and emotions into words that others could read and benefit from today. This is one of the writings of David that help me understand why it was said of him, "he was a man after God's own heart".

What is it like to live in sin, to live a lie before the Lord? There is no peace in our lives when we are living in sin. When we confess our sins, we are agreeing with God, acknowledging that He is right to declare what we have done or are still doing is sinful. When we confess, we are confirming our intention of abandoning the sin to follow God more faithfully. Jesus was nailed to the cross, and our sins were nailed to it when He died. He came and died that we might have abundant life (John 10:10). Yes, ours sins were forgiven when Jesus died on the cross. We still live in a fallen world; therefore, we sin daily and must repent. The Bible tells us that the wages of sin are death, but the gift of God is eternal life (Romans 6:23). Our walk and right standing with God demand that we make no excuses for sin being in our lives. We must acknowledge it and repent.

Consider Psalms 32. Read the account of David's sin in 2 Samuel 11. Then consider the love that God has for you. See how David's experience can help you understand the great opportunity provided for all of us to live a more fulfilling and productive life. TGIF!

Father, I thank You for Your Son, Jesus, who died for my sins. Thank You for the forgiveness I have received because of His work on the cross. I pray You will help me to forgive others as I have been forgiven.

Study It

Scriptures for Study   Additional Scriptures Found

Psalms 32 (NKJV)
1 John 1:8–9 (AMP)
Luke 23:34 (NLT)
Ephesians 2:4–5 (NLT)
Romans 8:1–5 (AMP)
John 3:16 (NKJV)

What I've learned from this writing:

What things have changed:

I have learned to forgive others:

The woman left her water jar beside the well and ran back to the village, telling everyone, "Come and see a man who told me everything I ever did! Could He possibly be the Messiah?" ... Many Samaritans from the village believed in Jesus because the woman said, "He told me everything I ever did!" When they came out to see Him, they begged Him to stay in their village. So, He stayed for two days, long enough for many more to hear His message and believe. Then they said to the woman, "Now we believe, not just because of what you told us, but because we have heard Him ourselves. Now we know that He is indeed the Savior of the world." (John 4:28, 29; 39–42 NLT)

The Power of Your Testimony

❦

You have probably heard of the story of Jesus and the Samaritan women He encountered at Joseph's well in John chapter 4. It is a beautiful story, with many lessons. There is just one that I would like to share. Have you ever realized how important it is to share your testimony? And how much of an effect it has on kingdom building? In this story, we are reminded of two things. First, we need to see Jesus as our example, and second, as His followers, we should be striving daily to become more like Him.

During His encounter with this woman at the well, Jesus behaved in a way that was quite unusual for a Jew. In those days, it was not acceptable for a man to talk to a woman in public, and furthermore, Jews did not interact with Samaritans. Samaritans were considered half-breeds and contaminated because of their intermarriages and the fact that they served gods other than the God of Israel. We could say that Jesus crossed the line! As the conversation between the two advanced, it took a turn to spiritual things. Has that ever happened to you? Whenever this happens with us, it is usually not intentional, but with Jesus, it was what He intended. It did not matter that she was a woman; neither did it matter that she was a Samaritan. What *did* matter was that there was an opportunity to share truth and change her life, and He took advantage of that opportunity. He was not concerned about anything other than the person He was talking with.

Have you ever intentionally continued a conversation that was leading to spiritual things? Have you ever tried to change the topic, for fear of confrontation or debate on issues you didn't want to discuss at the time? Jesus made a point of going to the heart of the matter. He unleashed the truth in love. We are frequently faced with opportunities to witness or testify of the goodness of the Lord and what He has done in our lives. But we seldom take advantage of them. Whenever we testify to others, we are simply giving evidence and being witnesses to something that is true, publicly declaring a fact we have firsthand knowledge of. This is exactly what the woman at the well did. She realized that everything Jesus told her was the truth, and then she shared her experience with the entire village. She was so convincing in her testimony that they all wanted to see and hear Jesus for themselves. Isn't it awesome when we can share the truth and have others seek Jesus because of our testimonies?

You are probably thinking of excuses as to why you don't take advantage of opportunities to witness. What really keeps us from sharing our testimony? What hinders us from being a witness for Christ? Could it be we have convinced ourselves that others don't need to hear it? The Gospel is not limited to certain people. Jesus commanded us to go to all nations (Matthew 28:19). Could it be that we are not credible in our witness? If that is the case, we must live our lives before others in a way that will change the way they see us. Maybe another reason is we think some people are not ready to hear and receive, but that is not our call. We don't make that decision. Our responsibility is to give our testimony and then let them decide. Remember, we are only vessels being used by God. He does the work through us. All we are required to do is share the truth about what we know firsthand about Father God. He is so loving and kind that He has provided the power for us to witness and testify about Him. The power of the Holy Spirit who lives in all believers is the power that is also in you (Acts 1:8).

Jesus changed the life of the woman at the well that day. She rejoiced in what she had received and shared it with everyone she knew. They became inspired and wanted to experience the same joy and change that they saw in her. She didn't make a big speech. She simply told them what had happened and how she had been changed. Can you do that? I think so. She was not concerned about what they thought or how she would be received. She just told what she had firsthand knowledge of. The invitation she presented to the people was "Come see a man." They were given the opportunity to see for themselves and make their own decisions.

We must extend that same opportunity to those Father puts in our path and then allow them to make the decision. Why is it so important for us to share our testimony with others? It is not God's wish that anyone should perish (2 Peter 3:9), and we are the ones He is using to help make that possible. When we share and spread the goodness of the Lord, we are doing our part to increase and build the kingdom of God (Acts 1:8).

Just as Jesus defied the Jewish laws and customs of His day, crossing lines of social class, ethnicity, gender, and culture, you and I should never limit our opportunities to share our testimonies because of lies and misconceptions that the enemy has created. We must be bold in our sharing, always reminded that we have the power in us to do it. There are people waiting to hear your story. They are waiting to experience the power of *your* testimony. Don't make them wait any longer. Seize every opportunity, because even now, the testimony of the woman at the well over two thousand years ago is still having an impact on people today.

Father, I thank You for each opportunity You present for me to tell of Your wonderful and loving work in my life. Thank You for providing the power to be bold for You as I talk with others who may not know You as I do. I pray You will continue to keep me close to You as I forever proclaim Your greatness and sovereignty on the earth.

Study It

Scriptures for Study   Additional Scriptures Found

Psalms 9:1–2 (NKJV)
Joel 1:2–3 (NKJV)
Mark 5:19–20 (NKJV)
1 Peter 3:15–16 (NKJV)
Psalms 105:1–3 (NKJV)

What I've learned from this writing:

What things have changed:

What happened when I shared my testimony:

Additional Notes and Recordings

About the Author

The second of six siblings, Delores has always been a people person, interested in helping others however she could. Dee, as she is called by her friends, worked as an educator for more than thirty-four years. Starting from the bottom as a first-grade teacher, she moved up over the years, experiencing each level of the educational system, including several semesters teaching undergraduate classes. The joy of seeing others learn and grow has always been exciting and rewarding to her.

Dee's passion is women's ministry and resulted in starting SEE Ministries, Inc. in the late 1990s in Virginia. The acronym SEE stands for support, encouragement, and enlightenment. She has worked with singles, children, and senior adult ministries also. Other activities include prison ministry, hosting an online talk program for encouraging those entering ministry, and writing several articles for *Unity*, a local Christian magazine in the Hampton Roads area of Virginia. Dee is an ordained minister and loves to share the goodness of God with others. She is currently working on her second book, describing how God changed her life.

For recreation, Dee loves to sing, read, and do creative things. She makes encouraging and scripture-related notecards that she gives to residents in nursing home facilities. Her favorite time is sharing and being with her granddaughter and son.

Printed in the United States